Crescendo Publishing Presents

*Instant Insights on...*

WELLNESS

# Practical Natural Healing Tips for Vibrant Living

Leon Koenck, PA-C

small guides. BIG IMPACT.

Instant Insights On...

**Practical Natural Healing Tips for Vibrant Living**
By Leon Koenck, PA-C

ISBN: 978-1-944177-49-2 (p)
ISBN: 978-1-944177-50-8 (e)

Crescendo Publishing, LLC
300 Carlsbad Village Drive
Ste. 108A, #443
Carlsbad, California 92008-2999

www.CrescendoPublishing.com
GetPublished@CrescendoPublishing.com

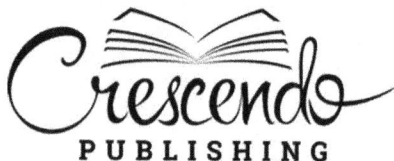

**Crescendo**
**PUBLISHING**

# What You'll Learn in this Book

This book explores how to become vibrantly healthy through making positive daily choices in the *Six Essential* areas for Life. By focusing on recognizing and evaluating your choices in each of the *Six Essential* areas and then moving towards healthier habits in each one, you will quickly begin to see remarkable improvements in your quality of life. Packed with practical advice on how to stay healthy in today's health challenged world, *Instant Insights*™ is your pocket guidebook for living, loving, and thriving.

In this book, you'll get **Instant Insights** on...

- The importance of eating healthy and what that actually means.

- That most of what we are sold as health food is actually harming us.

- What you need to drink to remain optimally hydrated.

- The importance of deep and restful sleep.

- The internal energy system and how it affects our health.

- Exercise and how we may be doing it all wrong.

- The ways our thoughts can have a direct impact on our health.

# A Gift from the Author

Communication is essential to everything we do in life. This book touches on some things we can do for our health, but really doesn't touch on relationships, which are vitally important for our wellbeing.

Take a couple of minutes to take this personality test, and then get anyone you work with, sell to, or even family members to also take it.

You'll get back a report that will give you some insights into what makes you and your relationships tick, and if interested, a link to a whitepaper showing the science behind this form of personality profiling.

You can access these complimentary bonus materials at:
www.bankcode.com/connected/whitepaper

# Table of Contents

# Dedication

I want to dedicate this information to my late mom and dad, who were always supportive of me. They were both robbed of years of living healthy partially due to a system that gave them incomplete and often harmful advice. Even though they had challenges, my siblings and I were always their number one priority.

I also need to include everyone's families and loved ones who have suffered, or left us too soon, due to listening to misguided information.

Together we can plant the seeds of hope and knowledge, so that our future generations can have a chance at a healthier life. Knowledge is power!

# Introduction

Do this, do that, don't do this, eat this, don't eat that and on and on. Where do you go to get unbiased, accurate information? It has become evident that the agencies we presumed to be protecting us have turned a blind eye to the people while they instead choose to support the interests of big businesses. Since you can no longer trust our watchdog agencies, then the best answer is for each of us to look out for number one – ourselves and our families. I am presenting information that I have personally experienced and can speak about from a practical viewpoint. As with everything you hear from anyone, you should always do your due diligence and run everything in life through your own filters.

I have been involved in medicine for over forty years, and have seen the tragedy and suffering that happens when we ignore our body's needs. So many people don't think proactively until they have received a diagnosis of disease or some other type of wake up call. I started in medicine with fifteen years as a paramedic responding to emergencies. Then I spent twenty-five years as a Physician Assistant working in small villages throughout Alaska, emergency rooms in Alaska and the lower forty-eight as a solo practitioner, and remote and rural urgent care centers. Early on I noticed how once someone was started on a medication, they would often need another in a year or two. It didn't seem to matter what they were being treated for (many patients were on fifteen to twenty drugs). For years I thought it was a good thing that we had these medications, and that we were able to get patients started on them, while not even considering they were actually harming the person.

In the mid '90s I was introduced to some energy healing that made a serious back problem I had much more tolerable. It actually allowed me to get off of pain medications that I had been taking for years- this was after multiple back surgeries and a loss of most activities I loved doing. I was able to start integrating these natural healing methods with my conventional practice over the years. In 2008 I was introduced to another form of energy healing called Bio Energetic Synchronization Technique (B.E.S.T.). I personally had a profound response to a treatment given in a hotel room, where I had volunteered to let someone demonstrate their technique to about ten people observing. I felt nothing and thought it was bogus, because he didn't ever ask me what was wrong. Talk about snake oil! Well, by the next day I had the ability to lift my leg to ninety degrees, where for at least twenty years I could never raise it above forty-five degrees. I had been to physical therapy aggressively for at least eighteen months for help, but was eventually told by the therapists and surgeon that I would never get that use back due to scar tissue from the surgeries, fusion, and damage done by multiple disc ruptures. So even though I couldn't answer why it worked in my logical mind, my heart told me to trust and accept that I don't know what I don't know. I became an Elite Master Practitioner for the Morter Health System, so I could use the technique regularly to improve people's quality of life.

I work in the emergency medicine arena, so it is not uncommon to have to use some type of medication to keep people alive or at least get them back on track. They have often exhausted all energy reserves and have created a perfect environment for disease. I have treated nearly a hundred and fifty thousand patients during my career and about thirty thousand of them with energy work or a combination. I am humbled all the time as I see the power of the body to heal itself. You have the ability to heal and live a healthy, vibrant life, you just have to learn that it is possible, and then apply the steps needed. My experience has also taught me that is is not the doctor or practitioner that does the healing. It is all about the patient, who has to unlock the power they already have within.

In this short book I will address some important areas we all need to work on to either maintain or regain our health. The good news is that every day holds the possibility for you to start anew and change the things you may have been doing that harmed your health. If your bodies can create a condition, it can 'un-create' it, as long as you can still reason, eliminate waste, and the body part hasn't completely shut down. Enjoy the journey on the road to vibrant health.

# Eating for Health

Food has become more food 'like' than real food grown as nature intended. To make food appealing and last on store shelves, the corporate conglomerates have opted to use toxic chemicals and added sweeteners to make sure the product will be appealing and that you will crave more. We can follow the increase of disease to our food industry. Interestingly, the start of heart disease closely followed the commercial processing of grain into flour. Heart disease was essentially unheard of in 1900, now there are over seven hundred thousand heart attacks a year- or about one every forty-five seconds.

Later, because of diseases being spread through unsanitary dairy practices, it was decided that all milk had to be pasteurized. This involved heating the milk to kill bacteria. Unfortunately, this also deactivated any beneficial enzyme the milk may have offered. Pasteurized dairy ultimately causes the body to become acidic and leads to an inflammatory response in the body. This is important because a major factor of heart disease is inflammation.

Cholesterol has become a buzz word, but mainly because there can be a huge profit on medications to lower cholesterol. I find it interesting that even though we spend billions of dollars on medications to lower cholesterol, the incidence of heart disease hasn't reduced even slightly. It has, however, been tied to an increase in diabetes, liver injuries and even a spike in dementia. A simple way I use to think about the damage done by cholesterol is to envision our arteries like a pipe. Rusty pipes typically have pits in them. Inflammation (acidity) leads to pitting in the arteries. One of the roles of cholesterol is to plug the pits before they leak, serving to prevent strokes. Dietary intake only contributes about 35% of the average person's cholesterol, with the remainder being manufactured by the body, as it is also an essential nutritional component of a healthy brain.

Diabetes has been known about for thousands of years. Over 90% of diabetes cases are Type Two, a diagnosis which directly correlates to obesity and a sedentary lifestyle. It is estimated that one in ten people now have diabetes in the US and that number increases to one in four over the age of sixty-five. The World Health Organization is stating that the incidence of diabetes is going to double by the year 2030. As you can see, the whole world is being poisoned in the name of profit. There are now over fifty *million* registered chemicals and countless others not registered (Some estimates are as many as $10^{200}$). Of these. only three thousand or so have been studied for their long-term effect on humans. Many of these get into our bodies via food, water, air, toothpaste, cleaning supplies, shampoo, soap, packaging, or cosmetics.

Now that we have identified a problem lets look at some things you can do to protect yourself. It is increasingly more difficult to know what is in your food or how it is prepared (or even know what country it came from).

An interesting observation that you may want to check out is the layout of most grocery stores; they traditionally have the organic foods on the outer most aisles. You can pretty much avoid all of the other aisles in the store, as everything in those aisles are chemical and preservative laden.

A good thing to keep in mind is that nature provides you with everything you need to thrive. So, consuming foods as produced in nature without any additional chemical is where you need to focus your food gathering. Eat foods that are organically grown, and have not been irradiated or heat- treated. If you can get to know the farmer, such as by going to farmer's markets, even better! Get your vitamins and minerals from nature as much as you are able. Fortified foods usually have minimal added value, and you can never be sure if your body will properly absorb and utilize a synthetic vitamin. Once we developed refrigeration, canning foods became a rarity. When we canned and fermented our foods we were able to get the natural bacteria needed by our intestinal bio-system.

A brief look at our intestinal tract is in order. Our immune system is supported by the nutrition processed and absorbed by our gut. It is imperative that you respect the gut, for it has been said that all disease starts there. Unfortunately, we tend to take our digestive system for granted, at least until it isn't working correctly. The intestinal walls are comprised of a very selective barrier that will allow a protein to enter into the body once a pair of enzymes match (one from intestinal flora and one from the food) and essentially provide the key. Over time, when exposed to inflammation, the walls become less selective and will literally leak into our system chemicals, proteins, and other by-products not designed to be in the body; rather these are things that should have been removed by the process of elimination.

Inflammation is the main cause of the intestinal walls being damaged. Things that damage the intestinal flora include all chemicals, preservatives, stress, medications even as simple as a baby aspirin- and some of the biggest offenders are antibiotics. You are exposed to antibiotics unknowingly via the foods you eat, even if you never intentionally take any. This can be the process that precludes allergies and even autoimmune disease. Autoimmune describes a process where the body literally attacks itself. This is thought to be triggered by proteins that were not fully broken down by the digestive process, which are leaked through the intestinal wall and 'seen' as foreign by the body, thus causing the allergic response.

Another cause of inflammation is the way meat is raised and processed. Animals raised on fattening substances that are not part of their natural diet leads to an imbalance of different oils and enzymes. The connection to red meat and corn feeding of livestock as a contributing factor to the development of heart disease is just the tip of the massive iceberg of the effect our altered foods have on our failing health. An unhealthy animal's meat and milk will also be unhealthy to us. The current widespread practices of raising, and mass slaughtering, animals create a disease generating mecca. If consuming animal proteins, you need to have animals that were raised naturally, slaughtered in a non-stressful method, and by-products processed via sanitary methods. A good rule of thumb is to eat no more than a deck-of-card portion of meat per day. This will help keep the body more alkaline, as it takes about four hours to breakdown animal proteins verses about forty-five minutes to break down vegetables. The extra acids needed to complete the breakdown of the animal proteins have to be buffered in the body, creating an additional stressor to our systems. Evidence supports that people who consume milk for years have a higher incidence of osteoporosis. Quite the opposite from what you see on television ads.

Other common health foods that are marketed as being healthy for you, but are indeed harming you, include whole grains (breads, cereals, crackers), vegetable oils (soybean, canola, corn, sunflower), gluten, corn syrups, most commercial juices (apple, orange, V8, cranberry), processed sugar including fructose, sucrose, cane sugar, brown rice sugar, beet sugar, high fructose corn syrup, date sugar, maple syrup, molasses, sorghum), artificial sweeteners (including acesulfame K/acesulfame potassium), aspartame (Equal, NutraSweet), sucralose (Splenda), Truvia (which contains other ingredients in addition to just stevia, principally erythritol), sports drinks, protein bars, soy milk, tofu or veggie burgers (anything containing non-fermented soy can disrupt hormones), processed meats, farmed fish (Tilapia, Salmon), all bottom feeding fish (mercury toxic), margarine, energy drinks, pre-packaged meals, pretty much every non- or low-fat meal or meal replacement, diet sodas, sodas, foods stored in plastic or cans, and on and on. As you can see it truly is nearly impossible to eat healthy if you shop at a grocery store or believe what the ads and magazines, even featuring supposed health gurus, tell you is healthy.

## *Your Instant Insights...*

- Eat a diet of 70-80% fruits and vegetables, of which one-half are raw and the other half lightly steamed (to prevent heat breakdown of live enzymes).

- Eat only organic and naturally raised meat.

- Eat balanced meals while avoiding large meals within a few hours of sleeping.

*(When making dietary changes, do it slowly!  Add some of what you are moving towards while slowly reducing what you are eliminating. If you don't, your body will reject the change and you will not be happy!)*

# What You Drink

As you have probably heard we are 80% water. Water is one of the components needed for intercellular communication (electrical conductor). Most people tend to not drink enough water throughout the day, and as such, most of society is chronically dehydrated. An interesting response we have to dehydration is we tend to feel hungry so we will likely eat, when our body is actually screaming at us to get more water.

Now, drinking water needs to be pure and chemical free. Many commercial systems put chlorine and fluoride in the water. Chlorine is used to kill bacteria and fluoride was presumably added to protect our teeth. We now know that there is no benefit to our teeth from fluoride, and it is highly carcinogenic. Old habits are hard to change, and fluoridation is one of them. Other things now present in our drinking water are chemicals and medications (birth control pills for example). There are estrogens and estrogen disrupters that are thought to be part of the current trend of girls entering puberty as young as age eight, and male sperm counts lowering around the world (this is happening is other mammal species too). Breast cancers, among other types of cancers are on the rise, and higher estrogen levels, and estrogen disruptors may have a role in their development. Certain plants that are sold as healthy drink options such as Soy are actually  harmful due to the estrogens they contain and the genetic modifications the plant has undergone. The chlorine in water is actually absorbed into your body with showers and hot tub use.

There are many theories as to how much water you need. I use the concept of looking at the color of the urine to determine if you are properly hydrated. If it is dark you need more water. You can start by taking your weight in pounds and dividing that in half. Then drink around that number in ounces of water a day. For example, if you weigh a hundred and fifty pounds you would divide by two and get seventy-five. So start with seventy-five ounces of water per day and then fine-tune it by looking at the urine. Also important is to drink small amounts of water throughout the day and not to chug down two liters before bedtime. For each caffeinated beverage you drink, you need to add an additional equal amount of water to offset the diuretic effect. I also encourage you to drink a large glass of water about thirty minutes before you eat a meal, as this will help your body send a full signal to your brain during the meal allowing for smaller portions of food to be consumed. Filter your water if you're not on a well. The best system to remove toxins is probably reverse osmosis. I personally use Nikken's Pi-Mag water filter system which uses triple filtration, magnetics and ceramics to create Pi water.

Avoid all sodas, and beverages with artificial sweeteners. Many of the commercial beverages we consume are high in sugar content, or have artificial sweeteners that are know to be neurotoxic. They also don't send a message to the brain to stop eating or drinking. The food industry has been putting excess sugars in beverages for years. Sugar has been shown to be almost as addicting as heroin, so it is no wonder so many people have to have their soda fix. Between the sugars and artificial sweeteners in our food and beverages it is no wonder obesity is so high. If you drink a single diet soda, or many of the juices, a day you are 65% more likely to be overweight in seven to eight years and 41% more likely to be obese. Along with the fattening of our population, we are seeing a huge increase in diabetes, heart disease and dental decay from the sugary, acidic drinks. The American Heart Association says that drinking just two sugary drinks a day can increase your risk of heart disease fourfold.

Limit caffeinated beverages due to the stimulation effect.

If you drink alcohol, remember there is a reason for moderation. We know that as little as two drinks a day can cause damage to the liver. The ethanol in alcohol breaks down into sugar in our systems, so it can also lead to weight gain.

# *Your Instant Insights...*

- Drink about one-half your weight in pounds in ounces of water daily. Filter your drinking and shower water to remove as many toxins as possible.

- Limit or avoid stimulating drinks such as alcohol, energy drinks, coffee and some teas. Instead, use naturally squeezed fruit juices without added sugars. They should not be concentrated, as those contain more sugar than the body can process effectively.

- Avoid processed dairy; substitute a non-Soy plant-based milk such as Coconut or Almond.

# Exercise for Health

Advantages of exercise include the elimination of toxins, the building of muscle, prevention of osteoporosis, and improvement in lung and heart function. Exercise has also been shown to be a great stress reducer and a solution to depression. It will help you think more clearly, and even help to keep dementia disorders such as Alzheimer's at bay. You can add longevity to your life span by reducing the incidence of cancers, strokes and heart attacks. Your skin will be healthier, and you'll even have better digestion. You can even use your improved self-confidence to create healthier relationships and even better intimacy.

Now, this is one area where everyone seems to have a differing opinion of what works best. Do you need to work out for thirty, sixty, or ninety minutes or more? How many days a week? Do you mix cardio with resistance? Do you do yoga or go to aerobics? What is Qigong or Tai Chi? Do I get a stationary bike, stair-stepper, or a treadmill? What about free weights? Should I exercise in the morning or evening? What about swimming? Do I need to take extra protein?

I want to share a concept that has been catching on over the years. The version I am familiar with is from Dr. Al Sears called Progressively Accelerating Cardiopulmonary Exertion or P.A.C.E. This method retrains your muscles to store energy in the muscle and to not rely on the burning of fat, which is required when the body goes into anaerobic exercise such as aerobics and circuit training. Sure, you will lose that fat with aerobic workouts and you'll feel good from the endorphins released. The body interprets this as a stress response, like you are continuously having to get away from danger, and will continue to store more fat for the next time you get into a fight or flight situation. With P.A.C.E. exercise you do from three to six sets of exercise utilizing any type of activity, from running, to weights, to stair stepper, to body weight resistance. You measure your resting heart rate and stretch then do a two-minute set of an exercise. Wait until your heart rate is no more than ten points above your resting heart rate before you do your next, more intense, two-minute set. You repeat this for a total of twelve minutes of exercise. You will continue to burn fat for twenty-four hours. When you are in good shape you can do three or four-minute sets, again waiting until your pulse is within ten points of your resting rate. You will also gain better lung function utilizing this method. Instead of jogging, which will eventually tear up your joints and spine, try doing short sprint bursts based on the twelve minute formula.

It is important to vary your exercise to include different muscle groups- as you may have heard, if you don't use it, you'll lose it. Also, you should continually increase your pace, intensity, and change the exercise routine to keep challenging your body.

Unless you are a professional athlete or body builder don't add too much protein. While it does aid in the building and recovery of muscle, it can overload your internal system and create more problems if you are not actively converting and utilizing it for fuel.

Yoga, Tai Chi and Qigong will all help to open your energy channels, improve your breathing and oxygenation, improve your posture and joint health, increase strength and flexibility, and balance.

Another often-overlooked exercise is simply going for a walk. A thirty-minute walk has as many benefits as an intense aerobic workout without the potential damage to your joints and energy reserves. Plus, if you can smile, be happy, thankful and grateful for all of the sights on your walk, you will gain even more benefits, as you will see later.

I am going to interject something about Vitamin D in this section, since the best way to get the amount you need is from nature-thus being out in the sunlight. So if you walk or exercise outside, you can be sure you get the amount and type you need. Vitamin D is used by every cell and organ in the body. Think of it as the key that will transport hormones to their desired target, and help calcium get into your bones. Recent studies have linked vitamin deficiencies to several forms of cancers (including skin cancer), heart disease, rickets, connective tissue disease, autism (when mom is deficient during pregnancy), falls, recurrent bladder infections, weakened immune system, skin disorders, depression, and the list goes on and on.

If you follow the official recommendations on the level of Vitamin D needed you would prevent none of the above diseases except rickets. Ideally, the level of Vitamin D3 in the blood should be between sixty to one hundred (sixty to eighty for most, eighty to one hundred if you have cancer or serious illness). You can get these levels by going out in the sun when the sun is at least forty-five degrees above the horizon. This is usually during the mid-day in most regions. In the northern latitudes, the amount of time available to get sunlight is greatly reduced depending on the season. For example, many areas of Alaska the sun is only high enough for three to four weeks a year. When the sun is at an angle less than forty-five degrees the predominate UVB ray will be deflected by the atmosphere thus reducing the amount reaching the ground. The UVB ray is more intense and will burn the skin very rapidly, so the most important thing is to not overdue it. You need to expose at least 50% of your skin to the sun long enough to get a color change (front and back), and then cover up. Be careful not to jump in the shower and scrub your skin as you can wash up to half the benefit away. If you can expose your whole body, do it. Most of the deadly skin cancers are found in non-sun exposed areas or in people who never go into the sun. Do not put on chemical based sunscreens as they will block the UVB ray and you will absorb the chemicals into your body. On the days you cannot get into the sun or it is the wrong time of the day or year, take an oral Vitamin D3 supplement.

The doses of Vitamin D3 needed that will promote health are:

| Infant | 35 units per pound of weight |
|---|---|
| Toddler | 1,500 units |
| School age | 2,500 units |
| Adult | 5,000 units |
| Pregnant or Nursing | 5,000-6,000 units |
| Adult over age thirty-five | 6,000-8,000 units |

You should have your level checked twice a year to make sure you are staying in the optimal range. It also helps to have some magnesium and Vitamin K2 in your diet to help the Vitamin D to be better utilized. Note that it is possible to become toxic with Vitamin D supplements. It takes a blood level of nearly two hundred, so there is a lot of wiggle room when taking supplements. The average persons' level will raise seven to ten points for every thousand units of supplement taken.

# *Your Instant Insights...*

- Exercise in smaller, shorter bursts to not put the body into a stress response.

- Alternate the exercise you do frequently and work all of your muscle groups.

- Go for a walk. Be appreciative of the things around you. Expose some skin to get your daily Vitamin D.

# The Body Electric and Using it to Heal

For a minute, imagine that our bodies are created by two cells - a sperm and an egg. From the union of these two cells a highly complex series of events leads to our amazing bodies that our scientists can't even start to reproduce. How do the cells know what to do? When to develop? What biological function they will specialize in? Was host (Mom) telling the cells it is time to reproduce? For the purpose of this chapter lets agree that there is an outside energy source that is sending the signal to the cells. We will call it the universal energy, as this process happens everywhere on our planet.

Within our network of cells, organs, chemicals, nerves, muscles, tendons, and ligaments there is communication between the cells and the command center, the brain. How vast is the capability of the brain to communicate with the trillions of cells? We know it is way more powerful than any computer ever built. Some researchers compare our conscious mind (those parts we are aware of and can actively manipulate), and our other-than-conscious mind (subconscious-the rest of everything that happens) on a linear scale. On scale, if you compared the conscious mind with the subconscious mind, the conscious mind would extend six inches around us while the subconscious mind would extend ten miles.

Based on this scenario, it becomes rather obvious that we are only scratching the surface of realizing the true potential of our brain power. Some basic examples of our subconscious brain functions include temperature regulation, breathing, digestion, glucose and hormone production and utilization, etc. You don't tell our body to do these actions, they just happen at the right time. I also like to believe that our bodies are perfect and they don't make mistakes, they just respond to what you give them to work with. This response is happening every second to second. The body doesn't think about tomorrow; it doesn't care about yesterday. It reacts in real time to keep the perfect pH (alkalinity/acidity balance), regulate temperature, process the by-products of digestion, produce the needed hormones and enzymes, remove waste, and deliver oxygen and nutrients to every cell in the body. There is no way you could even start to consciously tell your body to do all of these things.

The next concept to consider is how does the brain communicate to all of the body parts to make everything happen? We know there is a nervous system, but many of the nerves don't connect parts that interact. Some actions are even faster than could be transmitted via nerve to the brain then back to the muscle. Some researchers believe the signal could not be conducted through a nerve, so there has to be another communication network. Every cell in the body will actually generate a small electrical current. They also communicate via this electrical channel, so think of every cell as being a transmitter and receiver of a signal. Part of the electrical communication network relies on the extracellular (outside the cell) fluid to help carry their signal. So when you are dehydrated for example, it will negatively affect intra-cellular communication.

There is also an electrical pathway outside the body. We can now see this with sensitive equipment. It appears that there is actual communication happening in this electrical field that surrounds us. It is this pathway that allows for the extremely fast responses that you sometimes need. We can also measure this and see this field will become very weak when someone is under stress. This can be in the form of an illness, a disease process, or something as simple as a negative emotional thought. On the flip side, when someone is thinking about something that makes them feel good, or is in great health, this field extends further than most. An average distance from the body where this field is detected is about an arms length. Some can project this energy field ten, twenty, fifty and even one hundred feet or more. This might be demonstrated when someone enters a crowded room and you sense it, yet there is someone else that you never noticed at the same event because their energy field was low. You could relate this concept to your comfort zone regarding people in your personal space. When several people project positive thoughts in the same field, that field exponentially expands. This phenomenon may explain the power of group-prayer or directed meditations.

Energy medicine comes in many forms. Even though the energy techniques are different for each form of healing technique, I believe the end result is  similar for all of them. It is to remove interference within the body that is not allowing for internal communication between bodily systems and with the universal energy source. I also believe that the power to heal is already within all of us, you just need to learn how to access it. Part of learning to access our ability to heal is to first recognize and accept the possibility that it is possible. The next area is to realize that everything you put in your body has an effect. It is either supporting your health or degrading it. There is no in between.

Emotions and experiences from our pasts have the ability to profoundly impact our health. These past experiences at times become locked, like a program that runs on a loop always repeating. A sight, sound, smell or other stimulus can put our body back into the defensive physiology, as a memory pattern is activated that relates to to past experience. The subconscious will immediately go into the response needed to prevent harm from the previous experience as though it is a real threat now. Unfortunately, you never know this is happening in the background. An example might be waking up with a significant back pain although you are certain you did nothing to injure it. This is likely one of these memory programs that became activated while you were sleeping.

The process of removing energy blocks will start the path to healing and wellbeing. Some energy systems have the ability to find the emotion that triggered the body's response. Once the emotion is found, there are processes that can show the subconscious that the response is no longer needed. The body then will reset to current need, essentially shutting off that program. It is possible that there could be thousands of these programs running at any given time.

All electrical activity creates a current that can be measured. Any cell that transmits also receives on the same frequency. This leads up to the belief that whatever is transmitted is what is returned on the energy spectrum. You may have heard sayings such as Earl Nightingales' Greatest Secret that, "you get what you think about most of the time." Also, the Law of Attraction that has recently gained popularity says what you put out will come back. Napoleon Hill said that, "Whatever the mind can conceive and believe, it can achieve." These concepts have been handed down in literature since records have been kept. Thanks to modern science we are now better able to understand that there is indeed an energy created and received by the body.

We also know that outside energy interacts at our cellular level and with internal communications. Electrical wires, Wi-Fi, radio waves, cellular towers, and appliances are everywhere. The medical community has a billable code for exposure to other non-ionizing radiation, which encompasses all electrical interferences. There are people so sensitive to these interferences that they have to live isolated in specialized, shielded rooms. Even the electrical current running behind the walls in our homes are putting out a field that may be doing harm.

Children are the most susceptible to these radiation sources. It is estimated there will be seventy-eight thousand new cases of primary brain tumors diagnosed this year per the American Brain Tumor Association. Brain tumors are now the most diagnosed childhood cancer, and the second leading cause of death. Leukemia is the leading cause of childhood death and the second most diagnosed cancer. Kids should never be exposed to cell phones. All of us need to remove any wireless device from our sleeping areas and ideally shut our devices off as well as Wi-Fi base stations at night to allow a timeout from the EF radiation. A great natural defense against this onslaught is being connected to the earth. It acts like a grounding rod and can neutralize these harmful signals. There are even companies that sell a grounding sheet that you can put on your bed to allow you to be grounded during your sleep. This grounding also serves as a powerful natural antioxidant.

A fascinating experiment was done by Dr. Masura Emote in the 1990s where he demonstrated the concept of Hado. Hado is the power to dip inside into the spiritual realm to gain the healing and transforming powers of the life-force energy. He exposed water to different words either spoken, written, in prayer or in music, and demonstrated it was possible to actually change the crystalline structure of the water. The results were documented by a fascinating series of photos. When you see the power of these words on water, imagine how emotions may have the same effect on the water within our bodies. This is a profound thought that could have huge implications on our state of physical being.

We have also been able to prove that an emotion can have an immediate affect on the acid state (pH) of our internal body. A single negative thought will take a basic (alkaline) pH and turn it acidic within as little as ninety seconds. This negative emotion can be anger, fear, jealousy, worry, or even judgment. Positive emotions can have the opposite effect. Emotions will also affect the energy field surrounding the body, increasing or decreasing its strength based on positive or negative emotions.

Emotions are also known to have a direct impact on our DNA. The science of Epigenetics looks at what will turn a gene on or off. There have been numerous twins and triplets that were separated at birth and raised away from the biological mother. Following them for years has demonstrated that the sibling removed from the maternal environment rarely, if ever, contracts the genetic disease that they carry. The implications of this is that something external to the person activates the gene that expresses the disease or condition. So it may be the food they grew up with or the physical environment; but most likely it is their belief system. Worrying about, or thinking often about something can cause that to come about via the Law of Attraction.

All of our current medicine is based on a linear model of physics. It says that opposites attract, and for each action there is an equal counter reaction. What isn't considered in this model is the concept of Quantum. Where likes attract, and a simple action can have a resulting action at a distance through a mechanism known as non-locality.

Also, the current medical model tries to analyze the human as a mechanical unit. It ignores things that cannot be measured. Things like consciousness, intention, mind-body connection, and even the effects of emotions like love on the whole organism are not understood. Living cells have been found to emit a light via biophotons, and there are theories that some cells can communicate via the light emitted by the cells in close proximity and even at a distance. This is likely the basis for the aura around a person that can be seen by some people and by Kirlian photography.

Within a living organism is a lot of chaos. In the quantum world this is the natural way of things, but in the Newtonian linear model chaos disrupts and is not predictable, so it cannot be good. When you are in a disease state the predominate signal is one of the disease. It is non-chaotic. So the energy that comes back to the body is more of the same that supports the disease. To overcome the disease, you have to be able to disrupt the signal to one of healing and a healthy environment.

I have mentioned some of the aspects of our knowledge of the electrical body. We have just scratched the surface of the interactions and various processes that regulate us. If I left out a physical, or natural system, or energy source, it was not to diminish it; rather in this short book I want to get you to think and realize there is so much we don't know or cannot yet explain.

A way that all of us can help to stop negative programs from running is to add forgiveness and gratitude to our daily routine. An important step forward is to focus on feeling good now. You have heard that laughter can be a medicine. I have actually written prescriptions to patients to have them laugh out loud hysterically for fifteen seconds twice daily. The feedback from those that have done it is always amazing and positive. Another daily practice to incorporate is to look in the mirror and tell yourself, "I love you," and to mean it! I will list some steps you can do for forgiveness, with the idea being to stop the negativity associated with the past event. It is not to condone the other person(s) actions, but to free yourself from the victim state.

By offering gratitude for things in your life daily you are opening up to the beauty around us, and simply put when you are happy you cannot be sad.

Ed Foreman teaches that you have a choice every day when you wake up whether you are going to have a good day or a bad day. He has a menu that you can choose which way you want your day to be. When you take 100% responsibility for what happens to you in your life, you can control the outcome, and quit being a victim of events. You can indeed predict the future, because as you have learned you get back what you think about most of the time. Once you are able to tap into your passion in life, find a way to share your unique talent in the service of others, and then take action working towards your goals and dreams, then your future will come true as imagined. Remember, everything made by man was once only a thought in someone's mind.

The following tips will help to keep your energy balanced and help with positive thinking.

**Practicing Forgiveness** ©
(With permission from Morter Health System *www.morter.com*)

Identify and release a situation, action, or person you feel needs to be forgiven – an experience from the past, which comes to your mind often.

Having identified and thought about a person, action or situation, you are now ready to begin the steps of forgiveness. It is important to note you don't have to agree with the actions of the other person or the event in order to forgive. You are forgiving for your own sake, not someone else's. Until you forgive the past, this other person or event is controlling your life. This is true even if the other person is no longer alive.

**Five Steps carried out with feeling and emotion:**

1. **Forgive yourself**

   You must first forgive yourself for allowing the event to affect your health.

2. **Forgive the other person**

   Forgive the other person for any harm he or she may have caused you.

3. **Give the other person permission to forgive you**

   Maybe you did something you weren't aware you did. It is not recommended that the other person knows you are taking this step. You are doing this for you!

4. **See the good in the situation**

   Learn the lesson the situation taught you.

5. **Be thankful!**

   Be thankful for the experience and the lesson it taught you.

## The Morter March Release©

(With permission from Morter Health System *www.morter.com*)

These exercises will help to balance your body, improve muscular and neurological balance, restore symmetry to your joints, and improve coordination and stamina.

These stretches will also strengthen and balance muscle tone.

Here's how you do it:

- Stand comfortably erect. Alert, yet relaxed.

- Step forward with your right foot, keeping your left foot flat. Bend the right knee, so you can't see your toes.

- Stretch your left arm up to forty-five degrees. Your hand should be relaxed and open with your thumb pointing upwards.

- Stretch your right arm back to forty-five degrees. Your hand should be relaxed and open with your thumb pointing downwards.

- Turn your head towards your raised arm looking up towards the thumb, close the eye away from your raised arm, and STRETCH!

- Hold your breath for ten seconds. Think to yourself, *I am thankful and grateful for my perfect* _____. (For example: if you have a sore knee you would think, *"I am thankful and grateful for my perfect knee."*). (If you have lymphoma you would think, *"I am thankful and grateful for my perfect lymphatic and immune systems."*) Notice you never mention the disease or what you don't want.

- For the last two seconds close both eyes and think the positive thought.

- Exhale. Lift your arms up into the power pose (both arms raised up and think to yourself, *"YES I AM."*)

- Then reverse the process with your left foot forward and right arm up. Finish each side with the power arms up pose and affirmation, *"YES I AM."*

**Repeat the process three times, and do it three times per day.**

(Start your day balanced, sometime during the day, and before you go to bed.)

**Use Positive Affirmations**

I use the Morter Health Affirmation© daily
(With permission from Morter Health System *www.morter.com*)

Put this up on your bathroom mirror and say it out loud to yourself.

*Today is a great day, and I have the opportunity to show up as the BEST me ever!*
*My life is a HUGE success!*

*My beliefs create my reality.*
*I think big thoughts, relish small pleasures, and handle all things gracefully.*

*I am deeply grateful for all that I create and receive.*
*My life is now in total balance and...*
*I AM THE BEST!!!!*

*Your Instant Insights...*

- Identify, forgive, and release a situation, action, or person you feel needs to be forgiven – an experience from the past, which comes to your mind often.

- Do the Morter March Release©.

- Use positive affirmations.

- Go barefoot as much as possible on the bare ground. Try to get in two hours a day whenever you can.

# Sleep: An Important Part of the Day

We've all heard we need to get our sleep. Let's look at what that actually means. According to the National Institute of Neurological Disorders and Stroke, there are forty million people in the United States with chronic sleep disorders, and another twenty million experience sleep problems yearly. The U.S. Centers for Disease Control and Prevention (CDC) indicate more than a third of American adults are not getting enough sleep on a regular basis. Sleep disorders include insomnia, inter-rupted sleep, and excessive sleep. All of these can have a different cause, and all can harm our health.

Why does it matter that you aren't sleeping well? Your body uses the time during sleeping to rebuild and restore. We know that our immune system needs that time to remain able to fend off disease and illness. Our nervous system requires sleep and it affects our mental clarity. As many as a hundred thousand auto accidents causing over seventy-one thousand injuries, and over fifteen hundred deaths are a direct result of sleepy drivers. Lots of industrial accidents are linked to sleep deprivation, especially in shift workers that switch between night and day shifts. The cost to our society from sleep deprivation and sleepiness can be as much as a hundred *billion dollars* per year.

Many medical conditions are directly attributed to sleep deprivation: heart disease, hypertension (high blood pressure), stroke risk, obesity, lack of mental clarity, shorter lifespan, fetal and childhood growth retardation, loss of fertility, kidney disease, diabetes, Attention Deficit Disorder (ADD), depression and other mood disorders. In fact, you have a greater risk to your health from sleep loss than from smoking, heart disease or hypertension. People over sixty-five will have a fourfold increase in death from sleep loss.

Let's look at some causes that are known to disrupt sleep. Snoring and sleep apnea have a huge impact on sleep. Over 45% of the adult population are thought to have chronic snoring leading to increased heart attacks, strokes, and other brain related illnesses. Over twenty million people are thought to have sleep apnea, of which 40% are undiagnosed. This equates to 24% of adult men and 9% of adult women. Sleep apnea will lead to high blood pressure and a significant risk for stroke. Sleep deprivation due to snoring puts that person at a fifteen fold increased risk of having an auto accident. Daily stress can affect sleep. Alcohol and caffeine will disrupt our sleep habits. Poor sleep habits are another major cause. Some habits that are common include eating close to bedtime (two to three hours), using caffeine (half-life is eight to ten hours), or nicotine within three hours of sleep time. Avoid alcohol before sleep (it will initially make you tired, but as it is metabolized will cause arousal), avoid technology (no cell phones, games, TV as the light will bother you and often engages the mind thus awakening you), avoid irregular sleep hours, and too warm of a sleep environment (keep the bedroom cool).

An occasional disrupted night of sleep is not going to hurt you. People with hypertension though will experience an elevated blood pressure for a whole day with less than six hours sleep. Relationships will suffer for a multitude of reasons. If you snore or have sleep issues, there is a good chance that your bed partner will suffer right along with you. This can go on for a while without issue, but at some point it will become a major relationship stressor.

How much sleep do we need?

| Newborns | 16-18 hours a day |
|---|---|
| Preschool-aged children | 11-12 hours a day |
| School-aged children | At least 10 hours a day |
| Teens | 9-10 hours a day |
| Adults (Including the elderly) | 7-8 hours a day |

If you sleep two hours a night less than your body needs, you will have a fourteen-hour sleep deprivation in a week that you cannot recover. It will be harming your body, as demonstrated by the health and safety statistics we have reviewed.

# *Your Instant Insights...*

- Keep a sleep diary. Write down how much you sleep every night, and how you feel on awakening-are you alert and rested? How sleepy do you feel during the day?

- Take the electronics out of the bedroom.

- Go to bed the same time every day. Don't change dramatically on the weekends.

# Summing It Up

We have reviewed several aspects of what is required for a vibrant healthy life. What I hope you were able to to learn from your reading is that the choices you make are what will determine your overall health. No matter where you are in the health spectrum, you can make choices that will get you back on the road to health, or solidify your foundation. In reality, good health is easy to obtain if you know what to do, and act on it. When you look in the mirror you can say, "*You did this to me!*" Your body is designed in perfection, and only responds to what it is given to work with. So make good choices with everything that goes in, every day, every moment. Only you are responsible for your health.

We could not go into detail in all of the aspects of healthy living that were discussed. At the minimum, you now have some tips that can help you live a healthier life.

There are six areas in life that are essential to thrive. Dr. M. T. Morter Jr. taught me that if you can believe in our ability to heal from within, and you get out of your conscious mind, while following what he called the Six Essentials, then you can be healthy. We have covered these Six Essentials in the previous chapters. The commercialization of the agriculture business, the creation of toxic chemicals, and electrical interference has stacked the deck against mankind significantly. The US is one of the most corrupt nations in the world when it comes to the well being of its citizens, as it seems that money buys policies that benefit the big corporations while causing irreparable harm to the people. That is the bad news. The good news is that we all have the chance to live our lives healthily and happily. Since you determine your own future, you just have to make the right choices. You can live the dream of your choice, in good health. You just have to take the time to learn how to do it, and then put that knowledge into action.

You have learned that the body is electric in action, and that your body transmits and receives a frequency. You can have a direct effect on the frequency you are transmitting so you can receive back the same frequency. So you need to choose wisely what you are broadcasting.

You also need to maintain an alkaline internal environment. Disease will not survive in an alkaline setting, but will thrive in an acidotic body. This alkaline internal environment can be achieved though diet and positive thinking.

The current model of exercise is possibly not the best if you want to achieve longevity and have the energy reserves needed to move away from the stressful aerobic model of exercise and work out more efficiently. Something as simple as going for a walk each day can have lasting benefits to our overall health.

You learned that sleep is essential to a healthy life, and as little as one to two hours of sleep deprivation can have lasting consequences. Almost half of the current U.S. population has some form of a sleep disorder. Keep the electronics out of the bedroom. Keep a sleep diary and work on avoiding the things that can disrupt your sleep.

**Here are the Six Essentials for Life©**
(With permission from Morter Health System *www.morter.com*)

The choices you make in six essential areas determine whether you follow a lifestyle that results in permanent good health or one that can lead to distress, illness, depression...an unbalanced system that leads to disease.

### 1. What you eat

Your diet should consist of approximately 75% fruits and vegetables and 25% everything else. This keeps the body alkaline (its natural state) instead of acidic, and helps prevent injury and disease.

### 2. What you drink

Avoid stimulants such as coffee and alcohol. Drink mostly (natural, non-concentrated) fruit juices and pure water.

### 3. How you exercise

Get thirty minutes of whole body exercise done three times a week. Help your body stay flexible. You'll be surprised at how good it feels and how the tendency to suffer injuries is reduced.

### 4. How you rest

Good sleep every night is essential to your body's ability to heal and recharge itself. Avoid stimulants and heavy meals before you go to sleep.

### 5. What you breathe

Clean, smoke-free air is also essential to permanent good health. If you can smell the air you breathe, it is probably not healthy.

## 6. What you think

This, by far, is the most important of the Six! What you think about, you bring about. Think about what you think about, and cancel out your negative or judgmental thoughts with positive, loving ones. And, don't forget to forgive!

# About the Author

Leon Koenck has been involved in healthcare for over forty years. As an avid lover of the outdoors, he migrated from the mountains of Colorado to the beauty and ruggedness of Alaska. Previously an avid hiker, kayaker, spelunker, mountain climber, and explorer, a series of injuries curtailed most of these activities. He transitioned into clinical medicine from being a paramedic emergency responder due to physical limitations.

Working in clinics in small villages throughout Alaska, to larger hospitals in cities, he has been able to experience all types of home remedies and treatments, as well as witness the long-term effects of pharmaceutical medications. In emergency medicine, medications are often used to stabilize failing organ systems, allowing the body time to return back to healing. Unfortunately, many have never heard, or even had it suggested, that they hold the ability to heal within themselves.

The concept of energy healing and energy medicine were considered "snake oil," as they go against everything taught in medical school. Surely the medical gurus understand all of the ways a body functions and heals, and thus make sure students learn everything needed to help their patients, right? Once Leon discovered there were other methods that allow the body to heal without medications, he pursued these areas with a passion. For twenty years, he has been able to integrate different forms of natural healing within his allopathic medical practice. Now he has regular clients in at least fourteen countries he treats with energy work. He is also a Master Life Coach as well as a Certified Health Coach, and an Elite Master B.E.S.T. Practitioner. He continues to work in emergency rooms and urgent care medical facilities.

Leon's passion lies in helping people discover the possibilities they already have within them. In addition to teaching how to live healthy, he is also helping individuals, as well as businesses, learn to communicate more effectively by improving relationships while reducing misunderstandings. He feels that the ability to communicate can impact every aspect of our lives, including our health.

# Connect with the Author

**Website:**
www.LeonKoenck.com

**Email:**
info@LeonKoenck.com

**Address:**
5841 East Charleston Blvd.
Suite 230-483
Las Vegas, NV 89142

**Phone:**
1-855-800-9322

**Social Media:**
Facebook: leonkoenck, Butterfly Effect Seminars

LinkedIn: Leon Koenck

Twitter: @LeonKoenck

Pinterest: LeonKoenck

Google+ Leonkoenck

Local Impact Zone: Leon Koenck

# Acknowledgements

First I would like to give a shout out to my family for their support throughout my journey. Then to all of the people who I have worked with as patients, colleagues and trainers, which are too numerous to list.

A special thanks is due to the late Dr. M.T. Morter, Jr. for his wisdom and caring soul. He challenged me to stretch my core beliefs. If ever the phrase, "you don't know what you don't know" had more meaning, it would be when in a discussion with him. His children: Dr. Ted, Dr. Tom, and Dr. Sue for continuing the mission to improve the health of mankind worldwide. Drs. Ted and Tom have become good friends and have been instrumental in keeping me up to date with the latest breakthroughs and cognitions. Dr. Sue keeps me in tune with the spiritual path.

Ed Foreman and Earlene Vining for helping me to see that every day can be a good day, and reminding me that my choices will determine how my life will be. *I'm Alive, I'm Alert, and I Feel Great!*

Dr. Paul Scheele for opening my mind to the concept of whole brain learning, and to the vast, untapped potential of our minds.

Kevin Trudeau for the insight to provide a means, via the Global Information Network, for the average person to learn hidden "secrets" in a safe, supportive environment, which can help anyone who studies and applies them live the life of their dreams. Through the community of like-minded people found in the GIN Club, I have been able to travel around the world forming great new friendships. As Kevin says, "we'll see you on the beaches of the world." GIN has also allowed me to expand my natural-healing practice on a global scale, as well as learn about natural cures as experienced in other cultures.

Perhaps the most important person behind this book is Robbin Simons, for her encouragement and inspiration to publish this series. Her program makes writing a breeze, and has helped many inspiring AuthorPreneurs become published. Lastly thank you to the rest of the team at Crescendo Publishing for the artwork, editing, cover design and marketing.

# About Crescendo Publishing

Crescendo Publishing is a boutique-style, concierge VIP publishing company assisting entrepreneurs with writing, publishing, and promoting their books for the purposes of lead-generation and achieving global platform growth, then monetizing it for even more income opportunities.

Check out some of our latest best-selling AuthorPreneurs at http://CrescendoPublishing. com/new-authors/.

**Crescendo**
PUBLISHING

# About the Instant Insights™ Book Series

The *Instant Insights™ Book Series* is a fact-only, short-read, book series written by EXPERTS in very specialized categories. These high-value, high-quality books can be produced in ONLY 6-8 weeks, from concept to launch, in BOTH PRINT & eBOOK Formats!

## This book series is FOR YOU if:

- You are an expert in your niche or area of specialty

- You want to write a book to position yourself as an expert

- You want YOUR OWN book – NOT a chapter in someone else's book

- You want to have a book to give to people when you're speaking at events or simply networking

- You want to have it available quickly

- You don't have the time to invest in writing a 200-page full book

- You don't have a ton of money to invest in the production of a full book – editing, cover design, interior layout, best-seller promotion

- You don't have a ton of time to invest in finding quality contractors for the production of your book – editing, cover design, interior layout, best-seller promotion

For more information on how you can become an *Instant Insights*™ author,
visit ***www.InstantInsightsBooks.com***

# More Books in the Instant Insight Series

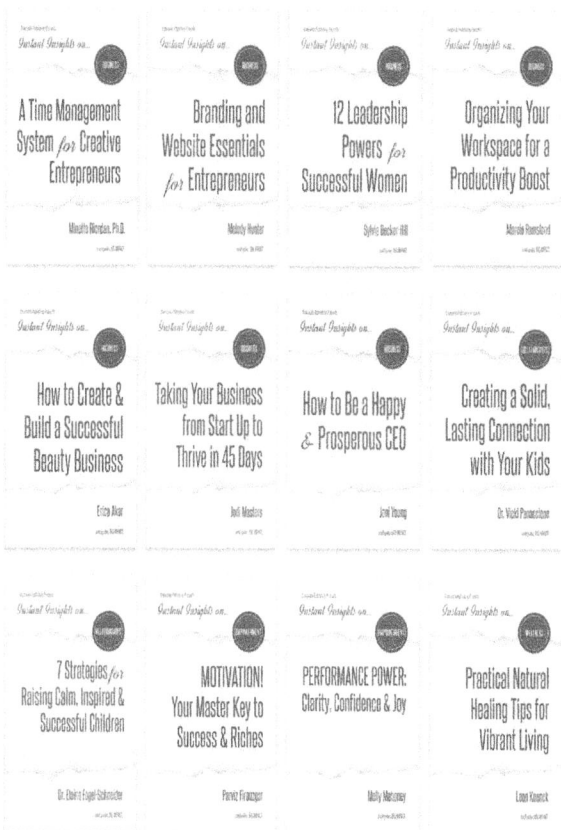

## A Time Management System for Creative Entrepreneurs
Minette Riordan, Ph.D.

## Branding and Website Essentials for Entrepreneurs
Melody Hunter

## 12 Leadership Powers for Successful Women
Sylvia Becker-Hill

## Organizing Your Workspace for a Productivity Boost
Mandie Roenbeck

## How to Create & Build a Successful Beauty Business
Erica Akar

## Taking Your Business from Start Up to Thrive in 45 Days
Jodi Masters

## How to Be a Happy & Prosperous CEO
Joné Young

## Creating a Solid, Lasting Connection with Your Kids
Dr. Vicki Panaccione

## 7 Strategies for Raising Calm, Inspired & Successful Children
Dr. Elaine Eugel-Schneider

## MOTIVATION! Your Master Key to Success & Riches
Parvez Firoozgar

## PERFORMANCE POWER: Clarity, Confidence & Joy
Molly Mahoney

## Practical Natural Healing Tips for Vibrant Living
Lani Kaurek

Crescendo
CrescendoPublishing.com